RAINFOREST

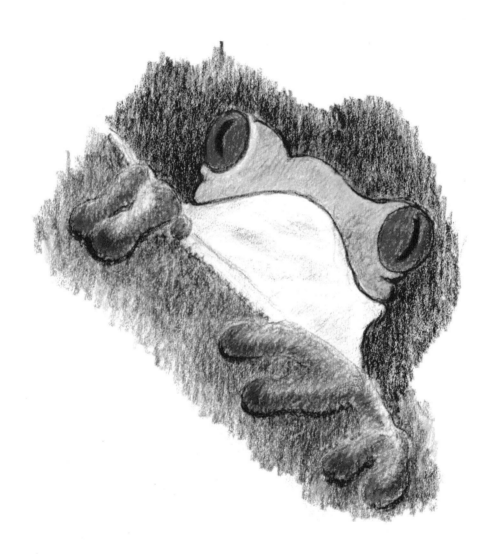

Illustrated by Mark Lerer   •   Haiku poetry by Caley Vickerman

Edited by Susan Newman   •   Foreword by Franco Andreone

© 2016 Frogs Are Green, Inc.

Rainforest Frogs

Illustrated by Mark Lerer

Haiku poetry by Caley Vickerman

Designed and edited by Susan Newman

Foreword by Franco Andreone

ISBN-10: 0-692-80932-5

ISBN-13: 978-0-692-80932-7

First Edition

Printed in the USA.

Table of Contents

Foreword

Rainforests always fascinated me. Since my childhood I've dreamt of traveling to one and looking at the canopy in search of strange animals and sounds in a natural three-dimensional building with all kinds of inhabitants. I'm sure this is due to books I've read, in particular those by Emilio Salgari, who lived in my hometown of Turin and wrote the epics *Sandokan* and *The Black Corsair*. Interestingly, Salgari described rainforests with an effusion of particulars, although he never moved from his studio. He took all the naturalistic details from the original diaries of Odoardo Beccari, a Florentine naturalist, botanist and explorer who lived in Southeast Asia, especially in Sarawak, where Salgari's Sandokan had his fantastic adventures.

When I became a professional zoologist and herpetologist, water always played a dominant role in my studies, whether as rivers, lakes, ponds, pools, or rain. I would spend night after night searching for amphibians in Europe. I searched for secretive spadefoot toads in flooded ricefields where Chernobyl produced its terrible clouds and rain. When the opportunity to explore rainforests finally arrived, I moved to Madagascar to do my field

research. Immediately I dived in among ferns and trees of incredible age and height. Touching these old patriarchs gave me a full sense of life, and many times I could feel energy flowing from me to them and vice versa.

It is common knowledge that in many parts of the world rainforests are shrinking at an alarming rate. In Madagascar, where I still go quite often, rainforests are cut for a series of reasons. Local people need spaces to cultivate rice and other crops and charcoal to warm their food and build their houses. The ground is so delicate that people simply cannot live too much on the same spot, and so practice a nomadic agriculture that literally destroys forests as it goes. At the same time the trade of precious wood essences, such as rosewood (locally named "bois de rose"), is generating a lot of problems and destroyed whole segments of forests.

Frogs, more than any other organisms, represent for me the animal voice of the forests, and so I accepted with enthusiasm the invitation by Susan Newman to write this foreword. Frogs are among those creatures the most sensitive to habitat alteration, and they are suffering enormously from the disappearance of rainforests. We have to do what we can to protect these biomes, although it is not always easy. One important way — maybe the most effective one — is through education. I believe that knowledge and education does not pass solely through antiseptic scientific papers and taxonomic discoveries, but also through pleasure and the arts. Advocating the preservation of frogs and forests through poetry is an important opportunity. I hope that the haiku in this book can be translated into songs. This would generate conservation waves that will help our beleaguered world. The only problem is time. In many areas of the world forests are being destroyed so quickly that there is virtually no time to save them. Education and international cooperation also take time, often much slower than the time of aggression and globalisation. To educate a child takes years, usually decades. For this we have to do our best to save forests and their creatures, and we must do so very quickly.

Franco Andreone

Zoologist, Museo Regionale di Scienze Naturali (Turin, Italy)
Co-chair of IUCN SSC Amphibian Specialist Group - Madagascar

Blue Poison Dart frog
(*Dendrobates tinctorius "azureus"*)

Toes as suction cups
My blue-ness warns predators
"Could be dangerous."

Blue Poison Dart frog

(Dendrobates tinctorius "azureus")

Frog Facts

Dendrobates tinctorius "azureus" is a medium-sized frog that weighs about 8 grams and grows to 3.0-4.5 cm in length. Females are larger and about half a centimeter longer than males, but males have larger toes. The frog has a typical lifespan of five to seven years in the wild. Its bright blue skin, usually darker around its limbs and stomach, serves as a warning to predators.

Amazon Milk frog
(*Trachycephalus resinifictrix*)

When I am nervous
Milk-like fluid pours from
My striped, bumpy skin.

Amazon Milk frog

(Trachycephalus resinifictrix)

Frog Facts

The Mission golden-eyed tree frog or Amazon milk frog (*Trachycephalus resinifictrix*) is a large species of arboreal frog native to the Amazon Rainforest in South America. These frogs are fairly large, reaching sizes of 2.5 to 4.0 in (6.4 to 10.2 cm) in length. Adult frogs are light grey in color with brown or black banding, while juveniles will exhibit stronger contrasts. As they age, their skin develops a slightly bumpy texture.

Yellow–Banded Poison Dart frog
(*Dendrobates leucomelas*)

I may be small but
My skin emits poison so
Do not mess with me.

16

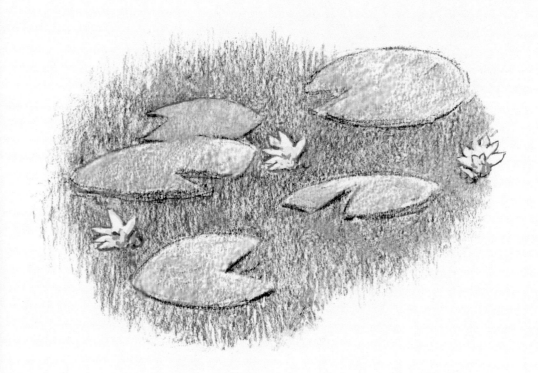

Yellow-Banded Poison Dart frog
(Dendrobates leucomelas)

Frog Facts

Dendrobates leucomelas is found in the northern part of the continent of South America. This amphibian is normally found in very humid conditions in tropical rainforests, close to fresh water. It is often found on flat rocks, trees, plants (notably bromeliads), and the leaf litter of the forest floor. During the dry season, specimens are known to congregate in damper places, such as under rocks or fallen tree trunks.

Northern Glass frog
(Hyalinobatrachium fleishmanni)

Translucent bellies
Males stand guard over the eggs
Keeping babies safe.

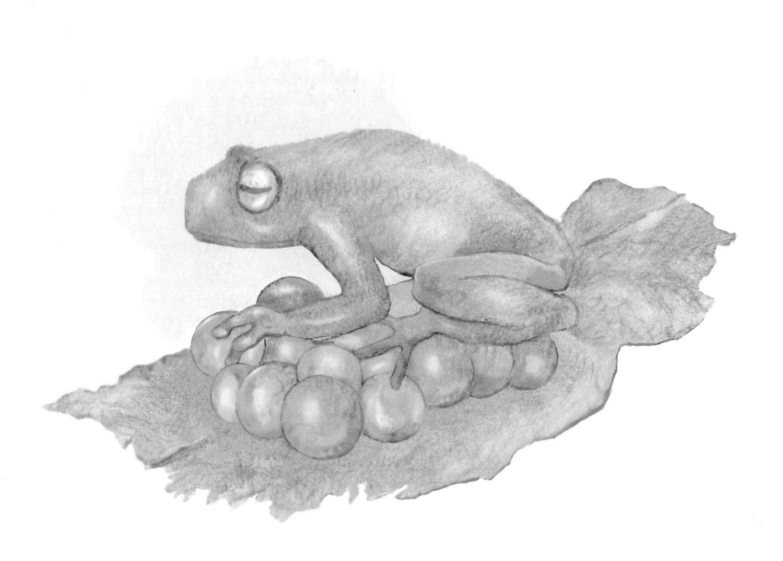

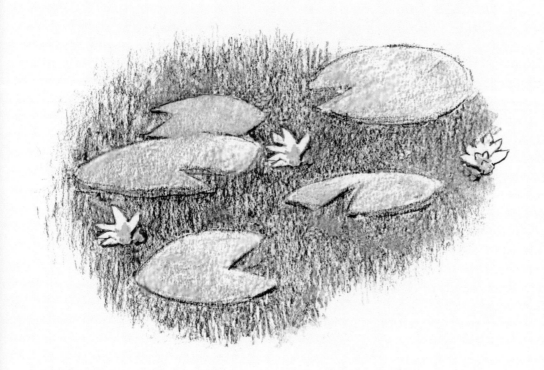

Northern Glass frog
(Hyalinobatrachium fleishmanni)

Frog Facts

The Fleishmann's glass frog or northern glass frog is a species in the Centrolenidae family. It is found in the tropical Americas. This frog's physical features include primarily green skin, pale yellow spots, yellow fingertips and translucent skin covering its stomach.

Glass frogs have similarities to tree frogs. These frogs tend to lay their eggs on lower branches, the bottom of leaves and near flowing water. The male frog stands guard over 18-30 eggs till they hatch and the tadpoles drop into the water.

Tiger's Tree frog
(Hyloscirtus tigrinus)

My markings are bold
But beauty comes at a cost
I am endangered.

Tiger's Tree frog
(*Hyloscirtus tigrinus*)

Frog Facts

Discovered in 2007, Colombia. The Tiger's Tree frog can be distinguished easily from similar species by the presence of a fleshy and prominent calcar tubercle and by its distinctive color pattern. The throat coloration is highly variable and cannot be used to diagnose any of these species.

Golden Mantella
(*Mantella aurantiaca*)

Madagascar born
Endangered because of the
Exotic pet trade.

Golden Mantella
(*Mantella aurantiaca*)

Frog Facts

The golden mantella (*Mantella aurantiaca*) is a small, terrestrial frog endemic to Madagascar. It may be threatened by over-collection for the pet trade.

The golden mantella is a uniformly yellow, orange, or red frog measuring 20–26 mm. The inner leg displays red flash marks. The tympanum is visible, but small. Brightly colored skin warns predators that the frog is poisonous.

Red-Eyed Tree frog
(*Agalychnis callidryas*)

Must be venomous
(That's what they WANT you to think)
Colors as disguise.

Red-Eyed Tree frog
(Agalychnis callidryas)

Frog Facts

The Red-Eyed Tree frog has red eyes with vertically narrow pupils. It has a vibrant green body with yellow and blue vertically striped sides. Its webbed feet and sticky toes are orange or red. These arboreal frogs spend the majority of their lives in the trees and are excellent jumpers.

They are not poisonous and rely on camouflage to protect themselves. During the day they remain motionless and all tucked in, so their green is hidden amongst the foliage. When it detects a predator, it abruptly opens its eyes and may startle the predator, giving the frog a chance to flee.

Flat–Head Bromeliad Tree frog
(Bromeliohyla bromeliacia)

All their tadpoles need
Is one banana-leaf pool
Filled with rainwater.

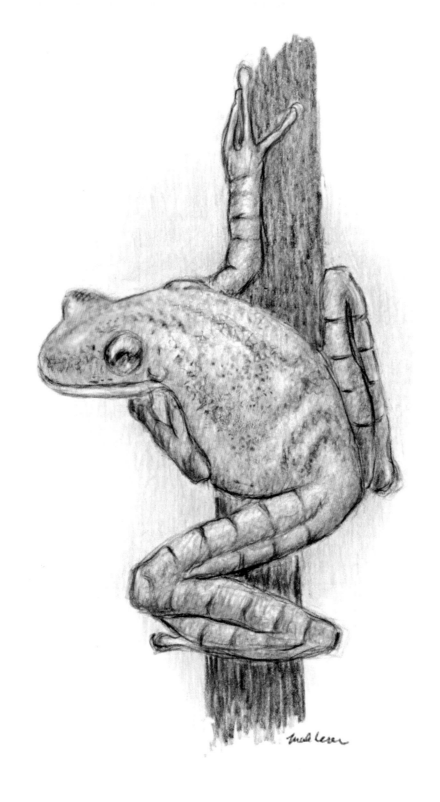

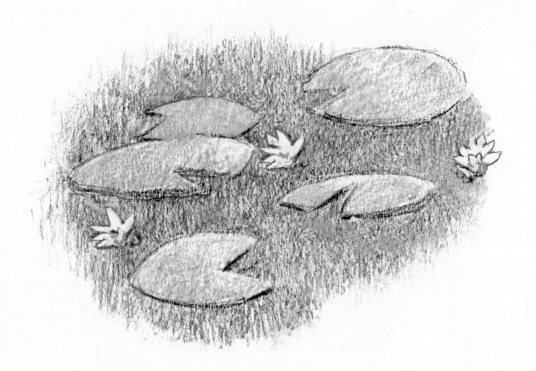

Flat-Head Bromeliad Tree frog
(*Bromeliohyla bromeliacia*)

Frog Facts

The Bromeliad Tree frog (*Bromeliohyla bromeliacia*) is found in Belize, Guatemala, Honduras and southern Mexico. These frogs lay their eggs inside bromeliads or other water-filled spaces in the canopy of trees so the tadpoles can develop. They live their lives in the canopy.

While somewhat of a rare species, these tree frogs have declined at higher elevations, possibly due to chyrid fungus. Deforestation and pollution are also a threat to this and other species.

Tiger Leg Monkey Tree frog
(*Phyllomedusa tomopterna*)

These frogs like the night
They secrete a waxy film
To keep their skins moist

Tiger Leg Monkey Tree frog

(*Phyllomedusa tomopterna*)

Frog Facts

The Barred Leaf frog or Tiger Leg Monkey Tree frog is a species in the Hylidae family. It is found in Bolivia, Brazil, Colombia, Ecuador, French Guiana, Guyana, Peru, Suriname and Venezuela.

Phyllomedusa tomopterna requires a pristine rainforest. This species is arboreal and nocturnal. Males call from trees or shrubs near ponds mainly between December and May. Clutches are deposited in leaf nests over ponds. Tadpoles fall into the water after hatching, where they develop until metamorphosis.

Rabbs Fringe–Limbed Tree frog (Toughie)

(Ecnomiohyla rabborum)

For nine years he searched
Calling out for his own kind
In the end, silence.

Rabbs Fringe-Limbed Tree frog (Toughie)

(*Ecnomiohyla rabborum*)

Frog Facts

The world's last known Rabbs' Fringe-Limbed Tree frog, a male known as "Toughie," has died.

The tiny animal was collected during a frog rescue mission in Panama back in 2005, a time when the deadly chytrid fungus was decimating amphibian populations in the region. Scientists had hoped to find a mate for the lonesome frog, but were unsuccessful. There's a chance that another Rabbs' frog could be found in the future. These animals are known to inhabit the high canopy.

Caley Vickerman believes in the power of play to transform our communities into safer and more joyful places. She is the founder of Guerilla Haiku Movement (ghm575.org), a community dialogue tool that uses haiku poetry as the means to start meaningful conversations with our neighborhoods, ourselves and each other. Haiku as a short and structured poetry form is easily accessible to writers and non-writers alike, and she is constantly delighted by the ways in which haiku's brevity forces a writer to get right to the point in poignant and beautiful ways. It has been a joy to discover frogs and find a way to tell each species' unique story in seventeen syllables. To Haiku AND Frogs!

Mark Lerer holds an M.F.A. from the New York Academy of Art and has exhibited his drawings at New York City's Nexus Gallery, Broome Street Gallery, and Lincoln Center. His cartoon illustrations have appeared in the *New York Post*, and he entertains his Facebook friends with the adventures of The Little General (based on a concept by writer Andrew Coe). His work on *Rainforest Frogs* is the beginning of a new awareness of environmental issues and the artistic challenges of drawing rare and exotic species. Visit: MarkLerer.com

Susan Newman is an award winning brand visibility designer and the CEO of Susan Newman Design, Inc. and founder of Frogs Are Green, Inc., a New Jersey nonprofit organization. She is a graduate of the School of Visual Arts (communication arts), The New School (web design), and New Jersey Learns (sustainability).

When Susan is not spreading awareness about why we should save frogs and amphibians, she's branding, broadcasting and supporting other creative entrepreneurs and organizations. Visit FrogsAreGreen.org and SusanNewmanDesign.com

Franco Andreone is a zoologist and the curator at Museo Regionale di Scienze Naturali in Torino, Italy. He conducts frog research in many places, including the beautiful and threatened rainforests of Madagascar, where he also acts as the chair for the IUCN SSC Amphibian Specialist Group. He is also coordinating the Sahonagasy Action Plan for the conservation of the 300+ frog species of Madagascar.

Other books published by Frogs Are Green, Inc.

Frogs, Amphibians and Their Threatened Environment –
Discovery and Expression Through Art (K-3)
by Susan Newman

Published by MyFatFox.co.uk for Frogs Are Green, Inc.

Frog Art Coloring Book - Volume One

Printed in Great Britain
by Amazon

75528107R00029